Say Yes to Self-Control

The Elusive Secret to Making Discipline Your Unconscious Ally

By Sensei Paul David

Copyright Page

Say Yes to Self-Control: The Elusive Secret to Making Discipline Your Unconscious Ally, by Sensei Paul David

Copyright © 2022

All rights reserved.

978-1-77848-056-0 SSD_Say Yes To Self-Control_Ingram_Paperback

978-1-77848-055-3 SSD_Say Yes To Self-Control_Amazon_PaperbackBook

978-1-77848-054-6 SSD_Say Yes To Self-Control_Amazon_eBook

This book is not authorized for free distribution copying.

www.senseipublishing.com

@senseipublishing
#senseipublishing

Get/Share Our FREE All-Ages Mental Health Book Now!

FREE Self-Development Book for Every Family

senseiselfdevelopment.senseipublishing.com

Click Below or Search Amazon for Another Book In This Series

Join Our Publishing Journey!

If you would like to receive FUTURE FREE BOOKS and get to know us better, please click www.senseipublishing.com and join our newsletter by entering your email address in the pop-up box.

Follow Our Blog: senseipauldavid.ca

Follow/Like/Subscribe: Facebook, Instagram, YouTube: @senseipublishing

Scan the QR Code with your phone or tablet
to follow us on social media: Like / Subscribe / Follow

Thank You from The Author: Sensei Paul David

Before we dive in, I would like to thank you for picking up this book from among the many other similar books out there. Thank you for choosing to invest in my book. That means everything to me.

Now that you are here, I ask you to stick with me as we take your self-discovery journey together. I promise to make our time together valuable and worthwhile.

In the pages ahead, you will find some areas of information and practices more helpful than others - and that is great! I encourage you to apply what works best for you. You will benefit from the knowledge that you gain and the ensuing exciting transformation of character.

Enjoy!

Table of Contents

Introduction **1**

Chapter One: Self-Discipline As an Ally **4**

    What Is Self-Discipline? 4
    You Do Not Lack Self-Discipline 5
    Instant Gratification: Enemy of Self-Discipline 7
    Advantages of Self-Discipline 8

Chapter Two: Demystifying Habits and Self-Discipline. 13

    Understanding Habits and Self-Discipline 13
    Ten Facts About Habits 15

Chapter Three: How to Exercise Self-Discipline Over Habits **22**

    Wrong Approaches to Breaking Bad Habits 22
    Forming Good Habits 28

Chapter Four: How Your Environment Enhances Your Self-Discipline **31**

    The Less, the Better 31
    Leveraging the Environment for Self-Discipline 33

Chapter Five: Leveraging Your Abilities to Enhance Self-Discipline **40**

    Simplifying Self-Discipline With Your Abilities 40

Chapter Six: Self-Discipline and Your Purpose **48**

    Discovering Purpose 48
    Simplifying Self-Discipline With Your Purpose 50

Chapter Seven: Self-Disciple and Personal Honesty **57**

Do Not Just Flow 57
The Moment of Truth 60
Reflection Time 62

Chapter Eight: Self-Discipline and Right Motivations .. 65

Victims of Success 65
Keeping The Light Shining 66
Starting Out for the Right Reasons 68

Conclusion 72
References 74

Foreword

One of the most important features of human beings that makes them different from animals is self-control. Animals are controlled by their instincts, which makes them act impulsively. The quality of our lives depends on the regularity of our ability to know when to restrain ourselves. This is critical in every area of our lives including our interpersonal relationships and career.

In Say Yes to Self-Control, Paul highlights the importance of self-control in our daily lives and how this helps us to live a meaningful life and achieve success. We would be happier and make fewer mistakes if we learnt to exercise self-discipline – choosing long-term benefits over instant gratification. This book is full of tips that can help you in this regard, which makes it another self-help guide from Sensei Paul.

Introduction

"You have power over your mind – not outside events. Realize this, and you will find strength.

Marcus Aurelius

John walked into his room that evening, struggling between reading his book to prepare for his upcoming exams or spending yet another night with his Xbox. This has been his routine for the last seven days. The thrills and excitement of tapping the buttons of his favourite game begin to overwhelm him. In the midst of that, the fear of failing his exams springs up in his mind but he soon brushes them off.

"But I have been playing this game consistently in recent times and hardly study for my exams," John said, to help

his reasonability gain ground on his persistent urge to play games when he should be studying. "Whatever will be, will be," he concluded, brimming with a smile as he picked up his gamepads and abandoned his books yet again.

I do not need to complete that story. You already know what will happen to John – failure. It is obvious to everyone apart from him. Many of us are like this in some areas of our lives. We know what we need to do to achieve certain results but we end up procrastinating until it is too late. You know you need to hit the gym and start your workout routine to get into shape but you would rather spend the time surfing the Internet. You know you should start cooking healthy meals to improve your health but the ease of grabbing something at the restaurant on your way to work has engulfed you.

You are not alone if you are seeking answers to why you indulge in unhealthy and unproductive habits when you know you should break them. This book is deliberately written to help you demystify self-control and restore you to the driving seat in your life. Practising the simple but effective tips in this guide will have transformative impacts on your life and has the potential to help you live the meaningful and successful life you desire.

Chapter One: Self-Discipline As an Ally

The level of self-discipline displayed by some people can be extremely impressive. Some people seem to have the superhuman ability to say no to their desires and focus on their goals. Yet, scientists have discovered that individuals with a high level of self-control have the same biological makeup as those struggling. This chapter will discuss the reasons some people display a higher level of self-discipline than others.

What Is Self-Discipline?

According to researcher Sasson, in 2016, self-discipline is the deliberate control of adverse personal performance. They posited that it is a virtue that creates the platform for an individual to achieve success and positive outcomes. In other words, self-discipline is tantamount to stopping yourself from hurting yourself. The truth about life is that we are the architects of our success and failure. Many people indulge in self-sabotaging behaviours due to their refusal to exercise self-control.

Self-discipline should be your ally. You should exercise it deliberately until it becomes unconscious. Once you make it your default response when you have to choose between instant gratification and long-term success, you should be proud of yourself. Self-discipline places you on a pedestal that sets you up for a meaningful and successful life. It is essential in every area of your life and that is why it is indispensable.

You Do Not Lack Self-Discipline

Chris: Wayne, my man. Anytime I see the features of Julian, I just want to have a piece of her. She is damn sexy. I cannot control my urge to have her.

Wayne: Really? Are you aware that she is HIV positive?

Chris: (shocked) What! Nobody told me! I better stay off that lady.

Just like Chris, it is not true that we lack self-control; we have just not found reasons to use self-restraint. Unless due to certain medical conditions, no human being will deliberately place their hands on a burning gas cooker. They know their hands would get burned if they tried it. This simple illustration shows that we all can control our actions.

No human being in their right senses would do things that would hurt them. This means that we create and imbibe bad habits that gratify us. Bad habits are not entirely bad; they also have ways to satisfy us. We refer to them as bad habits because their negatives outweigh their positives.

For example, alcohol is a depressant, which makes it capable of slowing down the nervous system. It releases dopamine, the feel-good neurotransmitter, encouraging you to drink more.

However, when you abuse it, it has several side effects such as liver damage, weak bones and muscles, amid other health issues. Therefore, quitting alcohol abuse is essentially a battle that involves choosing its positives over its side effects or stopping it because you do not want to experience its downside. So, ultimately, we do not lack self-control. We only refuse to exercise self-discipline over some habits because we are more focused on the instant gratification they offer.

Instant Gratification: Enemy of Self-Discipline

Bad habits offer instant gratification that makes us ignore their side effects or the long-term damages they can cause to our health, marriage, friendship, and career.

In the story of John, the instant satisfaction of playing games clouded his judgement, ignoring the impact it could have on his chances of attaining academic excellence. A cheating husband ignores the impact his action can have on his marriage while focusing on the immediate satisfaction of sex with another woman. It goes on and on.

If you analyze it, you will discover that there is a way a destructive habit gratifies you immediately you yield to it, making you ignore its long-term damages. Therefore, instant gratification is the anointed number one enemy of self-control. As mentioned earlier, we do not lack self-discipline; we only refuse to exercise it. Instant gratification is one of the strongest reasons you will refuse to show restraint when facing temptation.

Advantages of Self-Discipline

Self-discipline has multiple benefits when you exercise it. Here are some of them:

Achievement of Goals

Any dream that does not require you to exercise self-control to achieve it is not worth it. A 2012 study showed that self-discipline is a critical factor that enhances positive learning outcomes in a learning environment. The talent of Usain Bolt as an athlete is obvious. However, that was not the reason he became the fastest man on earth. Rather, it was his consistent training, which involves a lengthy 90-minute gym session thrice a week, that formed the backbone of his success.

Talent is never enough. Cristiano Ronaldo is one of the greatest footballers to have stepped onto a football pitch. Unlike many professional footballers before him, as of the time of writing this book, he is still playing at the highest level at the age of 37! Many footballers retire before then or step down to lower levels of the game. However, his physical fitness is extraordinary. There is nothing magical about this but his consistency in keeping up with a strict diet and training to keep his body in good condition. If you want to achieve and live your dream, self-discipline is a critical virtue you should acquire.

Maintenance of Interpersonal Relationships

Lack of self-discipline can ruin your relationship with your family, friends, and spouse. Your kids will not be happy to have an alcoholic parent. In the same way, your friends might stay away from you when you prefer to spend more time with your digital games and phone than with them. Andy Murray, a top tennis star, once had a breakup with his girlfriend because of the excessive time he spends playing games.

Good friends indeed stick with you through thick and thin. Yet, even good friends might abandon you when you have certain bad habits. They are not leaving because they are disloyal. Rather, they will leave because they do not want you to have a bad influence on them. Lack of self-discipline can also ruin your marriage if you are caught cheating on your spouse, for example.

Healthy Professional Relationships

According to a 2005 study, low levels of self-discipline lead to negative outcomes in personal and social life. Bad habits can ruin your professional relationships. For example, if you have a habit of not meeting deadlines, it will affect the trust of your clients and employers. This can lead to the termination of a contract. Trust is essential in professional relationships and no one will want to work with you if you lack integrity. Lack of self-discipline can also translate to greed, landing you in trouble with your boss, clients, and authority.

A Happy and Meaningful Life

Ultimately, self-restraint makes it easy for you to live a happy and meaningful life. Avoiding the side effects of unhealthy habits, such as health issues, divorce, loss of a job, loss of good friends, and the likes, will make you a happier and more fulfilled person. You cannot feel fulfilled whenever you remember the things you have lost due to a lack of self-control.

One of the best decisions you can make is to choose to exercise self-discipline during the periods you are tempted to opt for instant gratification at the expense of long-term benefits. It will help you to keep your job, relationship, and health. Therefore, to avoid living your life in regret now is the time to Say Yes To Self-Control.

Chapter Two: Demystifying Habits and Self-Discipline

Habits are like reflex actions – you do them without thinking about or controlling them. It takes time to form a habit but once it is fully formed, breaking it feels like trying to uproot a giant oak tree. Therefore, you must understand how habits are formed so that you can know how to break them and create healthy ones. This chapter will explore habits to help you gain more control over them.

Understanding Habits and Self-Discipline

Habits rob us of self-discipline. Sometimes, you have this strange battle within you where you know that you are indulging in a dangerous habit but do not know how to avoid it. You promised yourself that last year would be the last time you'd smoke but here you are smoking again this year. The lyrics of *Church* by Tom MacDonald perfectly describes this struggle:

I pray on my way

To the liquor store that they lock the doors

'Cause I'll lay in my grave

If the whiskey pours like it did before

As seen in the lyrics, you know you should not go there but you are heading there anyway, hoping someone will stop you on your way. You know you should not drink but you are hoping someone will stop you from doing it. It feels like you have lost the ability to control yourself. This is why it is better to avoid forming a bad habit because once it is formed, it becomes challenging to break it.

According to James Clear, the author of *Atomic Habits*, a habit is formed when behaviour is repeated severally over time until it reaches the "Plateau of Latent Potential." This shows the power of consistency. A drop of water per second over ten years can form a river. You should avoid something you do not want to have to become a habit in the first place.

The more you repeat the action, the more you lose your ability to control it. The human brain loves routines because it reduces the energy needed to process what you are doing. This is why you find yourself doing something once you "trigger" it, without processing it. The desire to satisfy your urge overwhelms you at that point, such that you struggle to consider the negative impacts of your action.

Ten Facts About Habits

To understand how to exercise more control over your habits, you need to understand these ten facts about habits:

#1 Habits are Not Permanent

It is factual that bad habits can be challenging to break. Yet, the good news is that they do not have to be permanent problems. Your ability to quit a bad habit begins with a psychological shift. If you convince yourself that you cannot stop yourself from doing something, your self-fulfilling prophecy will come to pass. Instead of saying "I *have to* smoke to reduce my anxiety levels," say "I *decided* to smoke to reduce my anxiety levels." This simple psychological shift will hand over the control of your life back to you.

#2   Habits are Formed Unconsciously

It is not the easiest choice to pick your habits. You can only decide on your actions and the decisions you make. For example, it was by choosing to drink as a stress management technique, on a day you were exhausted, that provided the avenue that formed that habit. That action does not become a habit automatically. It is consistency that turns the behaviour into a habit. Therefore, you can determine the habit you want to inculcate by deliberately choosing your behaviour.

#3 Every Habit Has a Trigger

Just like in stress management, you need to discover the trigger of a habit to start the quitting process. If you find yourself abusing alcohol after deciding to quit, you need to find the trigger. If you have used alcohol to ease your stress at some point, being stressed might be the trigger. In case that is the issue, you need to find other stress management techniques to make it easier to avoid choosing alcohol during those moments.

#4 Every Habit Has a Theory That Fuels It

Revisiting the story of John in the Introduction, we learnt that he gave in to his desire to play games instead of reading his book at that point when he said,

"Whatever will be, will be." Giving in to habits usually has a theory in your mind backing them. You need to discover that thought and counter it during your sane and calm moments. Remember the counterargument during the moments your cravings show up.

#5 Bad Habits Don't Die; You Only Replace Them

One of the reasons people struggle to overcome bad habits permanently is that they did not replace the bad habit with a beneficial one. The truth is that habits do not die. They have spaces in your life. Therefore, you must replace a destructive habit with a healthy one. to quit it completely. For example, you can spend the time wasted on social media to read a book. You will have to read consistently to make reading the habit that will replace spending time excessively on social media.

#6 Face The Unknown to Break Habits

Due to our innate fear of the unknown, we tend to make choices that are comfortable for us. Your habits are your safe zone. Therefore, it can be difficult to leave them in favour of new ones. The reality is that your habits satisfy your desires but you are not sure what you stand to benefit by trying new habits. For example, John is sure that he will enjoy the time spent on his game but it is not certain that he will pass even if he does read. Therefore, you have to face the unknown to destroy limiting habits.

#7 Breaking Habits Take Time

Many people give up quickly because they feel they are not getting the results they want. Habits take time to form and quitting them also requires patience. Do you remember the Plateau of Latent Potential? Habits are formed from the aggregate of several repeated actions.

Therefore, in the same way, it took time and consistency to form a habit, you will also have to be patient to break it.

#8 Habits Detest the Voice of Reason

Habits thrive on emotions because they are antithetical to reason and bad habits thrive in that terrain. Your cravings kick in and win the battle during the moments you are sad, anxious, or scared. Sometimes, they overwhelm you during the times you are super-excited. Slowly but firmly, let the voice of reason rise above your emotions to regain control during those periods.

#9 Battle With Habits Never End

The fight against a bad habit never ends. For example, even if you have quit smoking for ten years, you can still find yourself doing it again if you are careless. All that is needed is to find yourself in the wrong environment again. It will be as though you never stopped. Therefore, celebrate your victory over a limiting habit but never forget that habits never die. If you give them an inch, they will take a yard.

#10 You Need Help to Break Habits

The fact that you are struggling to break a bad habit, does not mean that you lack self-control. We all need help to be free from destructive habits. Do not hesitate to get as much help as possible from your friends, family, and experts.

Chapter Three: How to Exercise Self-Discipline Over Habits

When you cannot determine the habits you want to keep and the ones you want to quit, you are at the mercy of your instincts, which is not beneficial to you. The height of self-control is being able to decide what you want to do and the things you do not want in your life. This chapter will explore how you can create healthy habits and destroy limiting ones.

Wrong Approaches to Breaking Bad Habits

Our struggles with bad habits usually come from focusing on the wrong things. The two major mistakes in breaking bad habits are:

- Trying to change your habits instead of your mentality

- Trying to change your habits the wrong way

Trying To Change Your Habits Instead of Your Mentality

Your habits are like the fruits of a tree. The tree comprises your belief system, worldview, and identity. Bad fruits are products of a bad tree. Destroying the fruits of a tree you do not want is a useless activity. As long as the tree remains, it will always produce the fruits in its season. So, the common sense approach would be to destroy the tree if you want to put a permanent end to the fruits.

In the same way, you cannot quit a habit without a corresponding change in the thought process that birthed it. Your habits are products of your identity. If you see yourself as an athlete, it becomes less challenging to commit to a daily workout routine. That might also make you more careful about your consumption of alcohol and other drugs because you do not want them to affect your performance. This identity also makes it crucial for you to eat healthily.

Also, if you see yourself as a writer, you will have fewer struggles reading books because you understand that the depth of your articles and books depends on the quality and quantity of knowledge you have at your disposal. As mentioned earlier, habits are powered by theories. You have certain things in your mind that make it challenging for you to let go of a limiting habit. It might be the fact that you are focused on the instant gratification it offers or you are leaving things to chance by thinking you will be fine, despite indulging in the habit. So, you need to analyze your thought process regarding a habit to discover its fuel.

Trying to Change Your Habits the Wrong Way

Discovering the theories that power your habits is a step in the right direction. Yet, it is not all you need to quit a destructive habit. Below are some of the incorrect ways people try to change a habit:

Lack of Patience

The modern world is full of several innovations and technologies that offer easier and sleeker ways to complete various tasks. This is commendable and helpful. However, it has made many individuals impatient, with no regard for process. There are some things that we cannot speed up, despite our technological advancements. For example, we cannot make a pregnant woman deliver a child after two months. We have to wait for nine months or so.

Your habits are formed over time. Therefore, we can only quit them, completely, over time. Like a child, you will crawl, stand, and walk before running. You must make up your mind to quit a habit. Yet, a sheer determination is not enough. You cannot eliminate or speed up the process. This realization will make you less frustrated and disappointed. It will help you keep your focus and retain your love for yourself, especially on those days you stumble.

Overconfidence

Another issue that makes people struggle to break bad habits is overconfidence. Such people will not seek help because they are convinced of their abilities to overcome their habits. One of the facts about habits, that we mentioned in chapter two, is that you need help to quit them, especially the destructive ones. Therefore, you should not hesitate to get the help of professionals and your loved ones to regain control over a habit.

Low Self-Esteem

Overconfidence is one issue; low self-esteem is another. You should not allow the embarrassments you have suffered because of a habit, to make you feel that you do not have what it takes to break it. Remember that you do not lack self-control; you only need enough motivation and understanding to exercise it. You have already lost the battle against a limiting habit when you believe that you cannot win. Remember that habits are not permanent if you do not want them to have a state of permanence in your life.

Trying To Impress

The modern world is full of people trying to outdo themselves. Many people have lost the virtue of growing in silence without pressure, especially due to the advent of social media. Everything about your life should not be on the Internet. It was this lack of discretion that landed Kurt Zouma, a French player plying his trade with West Ham United, in hot water. He kicked his cat and the video was posted on social media. Consequently, he was fined £250,000 and he lost his sponsorship deal with Adidas.

It was a wrong move but no one would have known if it was not posted on the Internet. It is not recommended to turn your bid to quit a habit into a show for others. It will put unnecessary pressure on you and your show will be over the moment you stumble. Grow, learn, and develop in peace, without putting pressure on yourself to achieve lasting results.

Forming Good Habits

Good habits are the opposites and replacements of bad habits. Eating healthily replaces binge eating and other unhealthy eating habits. Daily exercise is a replacement for the failure to keep yourself in shape. Therefore, the best way to quit bad habits is to form healthy ones. The following tips will help you in this regard:

Determine Your Identity

As mentioned earlier, your identity determines the habits you can keep and the ones you should quit. How do you perceive yourself? An athlete, business tycoon, motivational speaker, or music star? Your perception of yourself will inform your habits. You cannot have a full understanding of the implication of a habit unless you have a clear idea of how it can help you become the man or woman of your dreams.

Set Targets

Self-discovery will make you set goals, which require certain habits. If you intend to start a global brand, you will have to take time out to study the market and products that will increase your chances of success. Your habits revolve around your identity and goals. When you have specific targets you want to achieve, you will have to form habits that will make them attainable.

Leverage Accountability

You need help to break bad habits and you also need help to form healthy ones. One of the ways you can get the help of others to form good habits is to inform a person you respect about your new habits. This external motivation can give you the extra impetus to keep your focus.

Chapter Four: How Your Environment Enhances Your Self-Discipline

One of the ten facts we explored in the second chapter about habits is that you need help to create and quit them. Your environment plays a crucial role in this regard. Your environment includes your physical surroundings and the people you have around you. This chapter will discuss how you can leverage your environment to create healthy habits and quit destructive ones.

The Less, the Better

Your ability to exercise self-control is strengthened when you do not have to use it frequently. According to James Clear, the author of *Atomic Habits*, people that have a high level of self-discipline are individuals who do not have reasons to exercise self-control repeatedly within a short period. Sometimes, we overestimate our ability to overcome certain temptations. The best way to avoid a desire or craving is to stay away from it as much as possible.

The reality is that we have moments of strength and weakness, which enhances or weakens our ability to withstand certain temptations. Note that every temptation offers short-term benefits, which makes it difficult for us to withstand them. As a human being, your instinct is to enjoy instant gratification even when it will lead to a long-term problem. Therefore, you should design your environment in such a way that you will not have to exercise self-control.

For example, there are times when you are not in the mood for sex. At that moment, it is more challenging for anyone to lure you into it. However, there are times you desire it; if you have someone that has been trying to make you cheat on your spouse around you during those moments, it then becomes harder to resist the urge. Therefore, you must set up your environment in a way that will make it easier for you to continue the right habits and avoid bad habits.

Leveraging the Environment for Self-Discipline

You can set up your environment to support healthy habits and prevent destructive habits by taking advantage of the following tips:

Leverage Exposure Therapy

Exposure therapy is based on behavioural science that in making it easy to find something around you, making it more effortless to do them. For example, by filling your pantry with fruits and vegetables, you can cut out the bad habit of eating sugary sweets. You have infused yourself with the energy and motivation to eat fruits instead of sugary sweets by making it easier for you to find fruits and more challenging to get sugary sweets.

In the same way, you can leverage exposure therapy by making all the supplies you need to cook breakfast, ready the previous night. When you wake up, it is easier for you to cook a healthy meal due to the availability of the things you need. If you wake up and feel too stressed to cook, you might end up opting for the option of picking up something in the restaurant. So, you must form the habit of stacking your environment with the things that will make it easy for you to create and maintain good habits.

Selective Influence

As mentioned at the beginning of this chapter, your environment also comprises the people around you. In fact, they have a stronger influence on you than you realize. Your friends and family can strengthen your resolve to break a bad habit and they can support your bid to form new healthy habits. Therefore, you should be selective regarding the people you allow in your circle and the things they are permitted to do around you.

You mustn't have people around you who indulge in habits that can stir up your cravings. On the other hand, when you have people who are consistent with certain good habits you desire, it becomes easier for you to inculcate the habit. Your desire to be in the good books of a friend, can fuel the formation of a healthy habit or lead to the formation of a destructive one. You cannot control the influence people have around you. You can only be deliberate about the kind of people you have in your close circle.

Habit Stacking

Habit stacking involves using an established good habit to trigger a new healthy habit. For example, most people do not struggle with brushing their teeth every morning. It is a part and parcel of our lives that is almost like a reflex action. Meanwhile, it was a habit that was formed through repetition and consistency. You can take advantage of this habit to trigger a new habit, such as reading your bible.

Consistency is the fuel of habit stacking. If you read your bible after brushing your teeth for thirty days, a link will be established such that you find yourself picking up your bible after brushing your teeth every morning. In the same way, you can choose to update your journal every evening after dinner. Ensure that you do not do something else after dinner, to strengthen the link. In psychology, this creation of a connection between two stimuli is called classical conditioning. It was discovered by Ivan Pavlov, a Russian physiologist.

Use Accountability Apps

Our phones have become essential parts of our lives in the modern world. We use them so much that it is difficult to imagine a world without them. The good news is that you can also use your phone to your advantage when forming or creating a habit. According to Nicole Forward of the Centre for Creative Leadership, one of the ways you can support the formation of a healthy habit is by leveraging an accountability app.

A simple Internet search will help you find numerous apps that can help you in this regard. Take advantage of it to build consistency and momentum. By recording or ticking your progress, you give yourself the sense of achievement, which gives you that feel-good sensation you need, as an incentive to keep going. It is an effective alternative to being accountable to a person. Besides, there is no crime or harm in using both.

Cut Out the Triggers

According to Sahar Andrade of Sahar Consulting LLC, you need to discover the trigger of a habit to quit it. When you do not know the trigger of a bad habit, it is tantamount to the lack of understanding of the source of a problem. Every habit has a trigger and you need to discover it to "switch it off." For example, pornography addiction has triggers. Giving yourself the license to stare at the opposite sex uncontrollably can be one of them.

Sexually explicit songs, ads, and videos will also fuel the desire. Therefore, the need to identify these triggers is essential. Cutting them out is tantamount to cutting out the fuel source of this habit. The same rule applies to every habit. Discover the triggers and deal with them. You might have to avoid visiting some sites or block some people on your social media page to reduce the chances of falling into temptation. Remember that reducing the need to exercise self-control is your best bet to enhance your self-discipline.

Chapter Five: Leveraging Your Abilities to Enhance Self-Discipline

You need to get to that moment in your life when you have a reasonable and objective knowledge of your strengths and deficiencies. This understanding is crucial to your ability to exercise self-control. In this chapter, you will learn how you can leverage the understanding of your strengths and weaknesses to create healthy habits and avoid unhealthy ones.

Simplifying Self-Discipline With Your Abilities

You can make it easier for yourself to inculcate certain good habits by aligning them to your abilities. The following tips will help you in this regard:

Strength Identification

You can indeed be good at doing anything when you learn it and practice it consistently. Yet, some things come more naturally to you than others. When you watch Lionel Messi playing football, he does things with the ball that you cannot teach people in any football academy. He has a natural talent for football that makes it difficult for anyone to produce the same level of excellence. Things might be different if you ask him to do something else. For example, he might still be a good medical doctor but never as famous and successful as he is as a footballer.

Since Messi has a natural football talent, the habit of training and keeping himself in good shape would be easier for him, than when he is expected to read every day, for example. On the other hand, some people find it effortless to read every day because of its importance to their natural ability to communicate and teach others.

Therefore, just like your identity, you must discover your abilities, which makes it easier to have healthy habits that give you a higher chance of success.

Recognizing Your Deficiencies

Just like your strengths, you should also be aware of your deficiencies. If you try to form habits that do not align with your natural talents, you will feel like a cat asked to bark. Doing things that are not natural to you can lead to poor performance and also the development of bad habits. Frustration sets in when you are striving but struggling for positive results, which is a natural consequence of doing things that are not natural to you. One of the easiest ways to limit your chances of success in life is to spend more time doing things that do not align with your strengths.

In the long run, this endeavour can affect your self-esteem because insensitive people would mock you and remind you of your failures. This rule applies to every area of your life, including choosing your hobbies. For example, I can play football to a very good extent. However, I am poor at volleyball. The truth is, nothing is exciting about the game to me. I would improve by playing volleyball consistently but it can never be like when I play soccer because football is in sync with my natural talents and passion.

Align Your Career Path

Your passion is critical to your career choice. You cannot afford to venture into a career path because it will make your parents happy. If you are not passionate about the career, you will lose the motivation and perseverance to succeed. It becomes likely that you will eventually quit when the going gets tough. Even when you are passionate about a job, you will still face challenging times that will make you question the reasonability of your choice. Yet, when it is your preferred career, you will take solace in the fact that you are living your dream.

Bad habits will creep in when you are finding it difficult to cope with your job demands. You will be mentally and physically exhausted consistently, which can tempt you to abuse alcohol or eat excessively as a coping and stress management technique. If you do not have a passion for taking care of people, you will be a disaster as a nurse. Find what works for you and make a career out of it. The modern world presents us with several opportunities to scale our businesses. Therefore, there is no skill that cannot be lucrative when you harness and optimize it.

Talk to Your Friends and Family

Your friends and family can help you to discover your natural abilities. They observe you and notice your performance when carrying out certain tasks. So, they are in a good position to help you to highlight areas of strength and deficiency. Indeed, their opinion should not be final. Yet, you can find helpful clues from their observations and remarks. As a teenager, it was obvious to my mother that I would excel in a career that emphasizes my ability to digest information seamlessly when reading and writing.

She would say, frustratedly sometimes, that all I know how to do is read and perform excellently academically. Some people excel in tasks that require dexterity but I have never been like that. You do not have to first waste time on a career path that will make you look average when you can focus on developing yourself for a role that gives you the platform to showcase your talent.

Seek the Help of a Professional

Sometimes, our friends and families might be sentimental when evaluating our abilities. Some people might tell you that you are average in carrying out a task because they are jealous or offended. In February 2022, Neil Warnock remarked that Caesar Azpicuelta is an average defender. Expectedly, many football fans, especially Chelsea fans, were outraged about the comment. Eventually, Warnock confessed that he made the statement because he was not happy about the goal Azpicuelta scored against his Cardiff side, which he felt should have been ruled out as offside. People can make sentimental statements about your abilities due to one reason or the other. Therefore, it is recommended that you seek the opinion of an expert if you are struggling to identify a career choice that aligns with your abilities.

Withstand the Siege

Life is an unannounced war zone. We fight endless battles in our minds against our cravings, plans, and the plan of others for us. There are situations where you know what you want to do but the people around you would not believe in you. My teacher in high school did not approve of my decision to apply for a top-class college because he was afraid I might not be able to cope but I did not back down.

Of course, he gave me the advice because he did not want me to miss out on the opportunity to get a scholarship. I appreciate the concern but I was convinced of my ability to achieve my goal and he was proud of me when I eventually got the admission with a scholarship. It is beautiful to have friends and family that support and believe in you. Yet, what you think of yourself is all that matters. Your success and failure in life are dependent on your choices.

Chapter Six: Self-Discipline and Your Purpose

Nothing beats the feeling of waking up every day knowing that it is another opportunity to pursue your goals. However, when you do not have a clear reason for living, all sorts of unhealthy habits can creep into your life. This chapter will discuss discovering your purpose for living, which motivates your self-control over certain habits.

Discovering Purpose

Concepts such as destiny and fate are too deterministic for the reality of our world. We cannot subject ourselves to the ridiculous belief that all our actions have been preprogrammed. Indeed, there are several coincidences and seemingly lucky circumstances for some people but they are usually products of the efforts an individual has been putting in before that time. In *Eternity*, rapper Dax said:

"They say leave it up to fate

Well, fate favours those who take"

The reality of life is that luck and fate only favour those who are willing to take risks to achieve monumental things in life. You need to get to that point in your life where you discover what makes you happy. Once you find it, design your life around it. Happiness in this context is not the temporal feeling of elation that you have, that disappears when things get tough. It is not as simple as having a good time watching a football game with your friends and family.

This is purposeful living based on the things that make life worth living for you. Some people, perceive themselves as legends when they can count the number of people they have impacted. This does not mean that you should live for others and neglect yourself. In *12 Rules For Life*, Jordan Peterson explained that we should learn to treat ourselves like a person we have a responsibility to look after.

He said this after discovering that many people tend to be at their best when they are given the responsibility of taking care of others but neglect their living conditions. So, you do not have to ignore or neglect yourself to make life worthwhile for others. Yet, you will find meaning in your life along the line of making positive impacts on others.

Simplifying Self-Discipline With Your Purpose

Unless you find something to live for, your life will be without a specific direction. You cannot identify distractions unless you have a goal. The tips below will help you to align your habits with your purpose:

Understand Your Purpose for Living

How do you want to be remembered when you are gone? How do you want to make the world a better place? Your answer to these questions is the anchor of your purpose for living. You need to have a clear idea of who you are and what you want to do with your life. The truth is that you cannot be everything and you cannot solve every problem in the world. Yet, you can try your best to contribute to your quota.

It is a clear understanding of the kind of impact and changes you want to make in the world that will make you stay clear of some habits. Life is worthwhile and meaningful when you live beyond earning money, catering to your needs, and retiring. This simplistic mindset will not allow you to create plans that will give others hope and add colour to their lives. How about planning to take more people off the street? How about empowering and sponsoring orphans? This kind of drive will keep you on your toes and make you stay away from some destructive habits.

Highlight the Habits You Need to Have

Your purpose for living will require that you inculcate certain habits that will equip you for success. Journaling becomes effortless when you use it as a tool for reflection, assessment of your progress, and planning to achieve your goals. Your habits are natural products of your interests, which reflect the things that matter to you. The reality that we will die someday, categorizes people into three schools of thought. The first group asserts that the fact that we will die someday should make us enjoy life while it lasts.

The second group claims that our mortality should make us seek ways to be productive every day to make the world a better place. The third group argues that the fact that our time on earth is temporal should make us productive while enjoying the moment. If you subscribe to the first school of thought, most of your actions are likely towards personal enjoyment, which can lead to uncontrolled indulgence. The second thought pattern can make you a workaholic while the third school of thought offers balance. You should enjoy your life but it should not make you have uncensored indulgence in habits that can ruin your health and your relationships.

Do Not Get Emotional

Some people make up their minds to quit certain habits and develop new ones because of the circumstance they found themselves in at some point. In some cases, it was because they were humiliated or experienced a divorce due to their failure to exercise self-control. The truth is that refusal to exercise self-discipline over your indulgence in some habits can make you break and lose the respect of your loved ones.

Yet, telling yourself the truth is what you need, rather than deciding to quit a habit because of how you feel at that moment. Such feelings are like the high people get from taking psychedelic drugs. It is temporal and never has a solid foundation that can sustain your desire to break a bad habit.

Do it Because it is Necessary

Some people make the mistake of choosing habits because their friends have the same habits. Of course, it is great to have people around us that can influence us to do the right things. Nonetheless, mindlessly copying and pasting is not recommended. For example, your friend might have a daily routine of practising yoga. This does not mean that it will work for you.

You might be better off practising meditation. These two practices have similar impacts on people but do not have the same procedure. Therefore, your habit should resonate with your abilities and purpose for living, rather than something you pick up to make somebody else happy. Before choosing a habit, critically evaluate its benefits and how it aligns with your purpose for living. This will help you know the right habit for you and the intensity of your commitment.

Determine the Relevance

The relevance of a habit to your purpose of living is one of the strongest motivations you can have to continue it. Critique a habit and the role it will play in your quest for success in life before committing to it. You cannot volunteer for everything. When you get your priorities right, your commitment will be limited to the things that are relevant to your purpose in life. This is the simple approach that can make you derive a sense of purpose and meaning from all your activities.

Chapter Seven: Self-Disciple and Personal Honesty

You cannot exercise self-discipline when you are dishonest with yourself. A life of pretence will make you pretend to have self-discipline when, in reality, you are deficient in the ability to avoid certain temptations. In this chapter, we will discuss the dangers of living a life of pretence and how you can turn the table around to boost your self-discipline.

Do Not Just Flow

Due to the topsy-turvy nature of life, sometimes, you just need to go with the flow. This means that you will not allow yourself to be caught in the web of anxiety over the things you cannot control. Yet, you cannot afford to go through life without a plan. It is not a crime if you were not able to figure things out early enough. Still, during your search, you should have specific things you plan to achieve, based on your current level of exposure and knowledge.

When you know better, you will adjust your current plans but you should never find yourself in any situation where you are confused because you have no idea what to do with your life. Confusion is usually a product of a clouded mind. It is a sign that you are unnecessarily emotional and sentimental about your choices. A confused state reflects that you need to choose between what you want and what you need. For example, you might have to choose between taking a lower-paid job closer to your family or a higher-paid job that will take you away from them.

What Really Matters To You?

Your choice depends on what matters the most to you, which should not be a product of that job offer. You should have decided whether making more money is more important than being able to spend quality time with your family, long before a job offer came in, demanding your response. Many people claim their priority is their family but they fail the test when it is time to show what matters to them. Honesty with yourself begins with determining what matters to you. It will affect your habits and it will reflect in the kind of decisions you make.

It will ensure that you do not pick up a habit out of the blue. It also makes it difficult for people to influence you negatively. Honesty with yourself gives you a sense of purpose and direction. You become your own person. It is your mind and only you can decide to be influenced by people that can add more meaning and progress to your life. The moment you lose this, you lose yourself. You will just swim with the tide and take whatever life throws at you.

The Moment of Truth

It is terrible to deceive others but it becomes preposterous when you get to that point where you lie to yourself. In that state, you start believing your hype and begin to think that your concocted image of yourself is real. In the movie *Rango*, the main character was found lying to everyone about his ferocious character. He claimed that he killed a group of bandits of seven brothers with a bullet to make people fear him. Luckily, a large bird terrorizing the town died while chasing him and he claimed the glory to become the Sheriff of the town.

However, he ran out of luck when Jake, the Snake, a scary outlaw shooting bullets with his tails, came to town. He was humbled and humiliated. It became obvious to everyone that he was not what he claimed he was. Lying to people can create a false impression that will make you bask in the adulation of your companions for some time. However, the moment of truth is around the corner. It will humble and disgrace you. You need to have a word with yourself if you have been fooling people because you cannot keep it up.

No More Lies

Do not visit the gym to post it on social media. Your body shape and physical fitness will eventually tell the story. You would suffer the same fate as people that do not exercise their bodies. So, what will be the essence of your lies by then? Why should you pretend to be an investor when you are not? There is no point in living beyond your means to impress people that do not care about you. When you have to pretend and impress a person to stay with you, it is a sign that the person is not worth your time.

You should value your friends and family. Let them know how much you appreciate their patience and commitment to you. Yet, you should never be afraid to lose anyone. Whoever threatens to walk away from you because of your current status, can leave. Such people will leave eventually, anyway Besides, they will pile up so much pressure on you, which can make you involve yourself in illicit acts that can ruin your reputation.

Reflection Time

In the words of Plato,

"An unexamined life is not worth living."

As a teenager, peer pressure got to me. I wanted to have a girlfriend so that my friends would rate me. I became rebellious toward my dad, to please my newfound love. It was a tough period for my family. In response, my dad would hit me and I got injured in the process but I refused to back down. I wanted to prove to him that

I had the right to live my life on my terms. I had developed a new habit of coming home late and everyone at home was worried.

All the efforts of my parents to get me to behave did not work out, until my moment of truth. One day, all alone, I sat down and reflected on my actions. I asked myself how this new habit would give me the kind of future I wanted. I realized that I would ruin my chances of becoming the man of my dreams if I continued on that trajectory. From that moment on, I started a new life. I ended the relationship and focused on my academics to the surprise and elation of my family. It was a move that paid off.

You need that moment of reflection where you evaluate your habits. Ask yourself some critical questions regarding what would become of you if you do not quit your bad habits. You will feel empowered to break any habit when you take time to objectively reflect on how it could ruin your life. It would make you seek help if necessary, to turn your life around.

Chapter Eight: Self-Discipline and Right Motivations

Our world is full of too many people trying to achieve success for the wrong reasons. This is why we have several examples of individuals who made it big but either disappeared or declined after that. This is also the reason some people become victims of their success. This chapter explores the importance of desiring success for the right reasons, to maintain your self-discipline.

Victims of Success

For the sake of respect, I will not state the names of the people mentioned here. However, there are several examples of people who began to indulge in destructive habits after they achieved fame and success. They have become the victims of their success. Fame and success do not change us but reveal who we truly are. There are some cravings you would not have because you cannot finance them. It is when you have the money to finance a desire but you did not pursue it, that shows that you can control it.

For example, it is challenging to be a cocaine addict when you cannot afford the drug. Therefore, do not be quick to judge others when you are not in their shoes. As a male superstar, many women would throw themselves at you. So, the level of temptation increases as we climb up the ladder of success.

Keeping The Light Shining

You need more self-discipline to *maintain* success than is necessary to *achieve* it. When you are successful, you have more friends and enemies, which requires you to be more careful because your decisions would attract more criticism than when you were at the bottom of the ladder. All eyes are on you and your mistakes will be treated as though you are no longer a worthwhile human being. Destructive critics will not let you breathe and your friends can even judge you wrongly when the spotlight is on you.

It is during that period you need to measure your actions carefully, especially when you are famous. One case of bad publicity can have very strong implications for you because bad news spreads faster than good news. People are always quick to believe false accusations about you when you are a star. It is worse now, in the days of social media. Before you know it, your name is trending on Twitter even when the news has not been confirmed. Your failure is a way to remind some individuals that you are a fallible human being and that is why it thrills them to hear unpleasant news about you.

Some people find it scintillating and exciting to find out that celebrities have issues in their relationships or marriages too. It is their opportunity to say mantras, such as "money is not everything in life" or "money does not guarantee happiness." Therefore, do not envy successful people. They are under more intense pressure to maintain their success and public appeal than other people. Your strategy to maintain your success is essential because things can change very quickly in life. If you are not careful, you will become irrelevant, despite achieving so much in a short time. People get bored easily and they are quick to seek the next new sensation.

Starting Out for the Right Reasons

The reason you want to be successful is more important than the fact that you achieved something phenomenal. When Barack Obama became the first Black American President, it was thrilling and exciting. It was an epoch-making event, making him a trailblazer. Indeed, the significance of his success in the fight against racism in the US was tremendous. Yet, his performance in office was more important than the fact that he won the presidential election.

Imagine if he used his power and influence as the president to persecute and oppress White people. What if he came with a revenge agenda to punish White people for years of Black slavery? His time in office would have been disastrous. It would have been similar to Adolf Hitler, the German dictator who leveraged his power as the leader of Germany to persecute and kill Jews, leading to a World War.

Therefore, the motive for seeking success is greater than the achievement of success. When you have the right motives, you will find it less challenging to exercise self-control when you are at the peak of your success. The following tips will help you in this regard:

Avoid Revenge

Do not let revenge fuel a new habit. When you are vengeful, your heart is full of bitterness and this can make you commit a crime if you do not control the urge. Someone broke up with you because of your shape; do not start a workout routine to get back at the person. It is pointless. It does not mean the person will still value you or regret leaving you.

Even if you have the body of an athlete as a man or the body of a model as a woman, a cheater would still be unfaithful. Disloyal people do not have concrete reasons for their actions. They do not act that way because of your actions or inactions. They are simply expressing their unhealthy selves.

Identify the Relevance of Your Success

On a personal note, I want to make a lot of money because I want to be able to help others. Some people need individuals that can believe and invest in their plans. I want to be the reason many people achieve their dreams and making money is critical in that regard. Take out time to find a cause that will benefit from your wealth and influence. This will keep you on your toes and motivate you.

Picture how you would use your money to make life worthwhile for yourself and others. Money will not make you happy but you can use it in a way that will make your life meaningful. It all begins by identifying worthwhile investments, the outcomes of which will make you have a sense of purpose and achievement.

Conclusion

We learn every day and I am convinced that this journey has added to your knowledge. Most importantly, I believe it has shaped certain aspects of your life and given you a clearer vision of the kind of man or woman of your dreams you aspire to become. If this has happened to you, I am satisfied. The essence of writing this book is to add value to your life and give you reasons to wake up every day.

During this journey, we discovered that self-control is not as elusive as most people think. We stated that we simply need to find reasons to exercise self-discipline and boom! We identified your abilities and purpose for living as two critical areas you need to discover to align your habits. This sense of direction determines the habits you should break and the ones you should create. We also highlighted proven tips that can help you break bad habits and create healthy ones.

Towards the end of this journey, we discussed the importance of being honest with ourselves. We also discussed the importance of achieving success for the right reasons. Many of the things you learned in this book might not have jumped out at you but they have the potential to help you live a disciplined and meaningful life. Practice them to experience the full force of their transformative power. The best part of your life is ahead of you.

- It's a great day to be alive!

References

Baumeister, R. and Tierney, J. (2011). Willpower: Rediscovering the greatest human strength. New York: Penguin Press.

Duckworth, A. L. and Seligman, M. E. P. (2005). Self-discipline outdoes IQ in predicting academic performance of adolescents. Psychological Science, 16, 939–944.

Sasson, R. (2016). What is self-discipline? Definitions. Retrieved 1 March, 2016 from: http://www.successconsciousness.com/blog/inner-strength/what-is-self-discipline-definitions

Thank you for reading this book!

If you found this book helpful, I would be grateful if you would **post an honest review on Amazon** so this book can reach other supportive readers like you!

All you need to do is digitally flip to the back and leave your review. Or visit amazon.com/author/senseipauldavid click the correct book cover and click on the blue link next to the yellow stars that say, "customer reviews."

As always...
It's a great day to be alive!

Get/Share Our FREE All-Ages Mental Health Book Now!

FREE Self-Development Book for Every Family

senseiselfdevelopment.senseipublishing.com

Click Below or Search Amazon for Another Book In This Series Or Visit:

www.amazon.com/author/senseipauldavid

www.senseipublishing.com

@senseipublishing
#senseipublishing

Check out our **recommendations** for other books for adults & kids plus other great resources by visiting
www.senseipublishing.com/resources/

Join Our Publishing Journey!

If you would like to receive FREE BOOKS, special offers, please visit www.senseipublishing.com and join our newsletter by entering your email address in the pop-up box

Follow Our Engaging Blog NOW! senseipauldavid.ca

Get Our FREE Books Today!

Click & Share the Link Below

FREE Self-Development Book
senseiselfdevelopment.senseipublishing.com

FREE BONUS!!!
Experience Over 25 FREE Engaging Guided Meditations!

Prized Skills & Practices for Adults & Kids. Help Restore Deep-Sleep, Lower Stress, Improve Posture, Navigate Uncertainty & More.

Download the Free Insight Timer App and click the link below:
http://insig.ht/sensei_paul

About Sensei Publishing

Sensei Publishing commits itself to helping people of all ages transform into better versions of themselves by providing high-quality and research-based self-development books with an emphasis on mental health and guided meditations. Sensei Publishing offers well-written e-books, audiobooks, paperbacks and online courses that simplify complicated but practical topics in line with its mission to inspire people towards positive transformation.

It's a great day to be alive!

About the Author

I create simple & transformative eBooks & Guided Meditations for Adults & Children proven to help navigate uncertainty, solve niche problems & bring families closer together.

I'm a former finance project manager, private pilot, jiu-jitsu instructor, musician & former University of Toronto Fitness Trainer. I prefer a science-based approach to focus on these & other areas in my life to stay humble & hungry to evolve. I hope you enjoy my work and I'd love to hear your feedback.

- It's a great day to be alive!
Sensei Paul David

Scan & Follow/Like/Subscribe: Facebook, Instagram, YouTube: @senseipublishing

Scan using your phone/iPad camera for Social Media Visit us at www.senseipublishing.com and sign up for our newsletter to learn more about our exciting books and to experience our FREE Guided Meditations for Kids & Adults.

www.ingramcontent.com/pod-product-compliance
Lightning Source LLC
Chambersburg PA
CBHW070313120526
44590CB00017B/2659